ALMANACS

Jen Hadfield lives in Shetland where she works as a poet and writing tutor. Her first collection *Almanacs* (Bloodaxe Books, 2005) was written in Shetland and the Western Isles in 2002 thanks to a bursary from the Scottish Arts Council, and it won an Eric Gregory Award in 2003, which enabled her to work on her second collection, *Nigh-No-Place* (Bloodaxe Books, 2008), in Canada and Shetland. She went on to win the T.S. Eliot Prize for *Nigh-No-Place*, which was also a Poetry Book Society Recommendation as well as being shortlisted for the Forward Prize for Best Collection. She has also received a Dewar Award to produce a solo exhibition of Shetland ex-votos in the style of sacred Mexican folk art, incorporating rubrics of very short fiction, and won the Edwin Morgan Poetry Competition in 2012. Her third collection, *Byssus*, was published by Picador in 2014.

Jen Hadfield's website: www.jenhadfield.co.uk

JEN HADFIELD

Almanacs

BLOODAXE BOOKS

ISBN: 978 1 85224 687 7

First published 2005 by
Bloodaxe Books Ltd,
Eastburn,
South Park,
Northumberland NE46 1BS.

www.bloodaxebooks.com
For further information about Bloodaxe titles
please visit our website or write to
the above address for a catalogue.

Supported using public funding by
ARTS COUNCIL
ENGLAND

Digital reprint of the Bloodaxe Books 2005 edition.

for Tash

and for their support during the writing,
my love and loyalty to

Charles and Bonnie Hadfield

Marie Carter, Anna Daintrey, Aviva Dautch
Alwyn Egginton, Linda Henderson, Tom Leonard
Andrew Miller, Janet Robertson, Gerry Stewart
my Jenny, Rebecca Wright

And Joan and Marguerite,
who should be dedicated a book
all of their own, but failing that –
consider this a great-grandchild.

ACKNOWLEDGEMENTS

Acknowledgements are due to the editors of the following publications in which some of these poems first appeared: *Avocado, Being Alive* (Bloodaxe Books, 2004), *Chapman, The Dark Horse, Heaventree New Poets* (2nd vol, Heaventree Press, 2005), *Island, Grain Magazine, The Fiddlehead, Hummingbird, Hanging Loose, Magma, Muuna Takeena, New Shetlander, The New Writer, New Writing 13* (Picador, 2005), *New Writing Scotland, Paper Tiger, Poetry Salzburg Review, Poetry Scotland, Rain Dog* and *Word Jig: New Fiction from Scotland* (Hanging Loose Press, 2003); a version of 'Marking' appears in *painted, Spoken* (5) and in the Poetry Library's website at
http://www.poetrymagazines.org.uk

The sequence *Lorelei's Lore* was written with the help of a bursary from the Scottish Arts Council. I blame Robert Alan Jamieson for the trip to Shetland. Linda Henderson midwifed all the poems in Skye. And none would appear in book form were it not for the help of Roddy Lumsden.

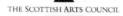
THE SCOTTISH ARTS COUNCIL

CONTENTS

Ashley Farm

When I lift my bottle
she looks up, a sure poem
with a skull like quartzrock.
She plays her tail xylophone
across byre bars.
She hooks her tail
in a high crozier, to shit.

Melodeon on the Road Home

(for Jenny)

I love your slut dog,
as silent with his three print spots
as a musical primer.
He sags like a melodeon
across my spread knees.
When I dig my fingers
into the butterfly hollows
in his chest, he pushes my breasts
apart with stiff legs.
Isn't it good
to forget you're anything but fat
and bone? I'm telling you
it's good to be hearing your dog's tune
on the broad curve out of town,
a poem starting,
pattering the breathless little keys.
To see more than me, I flick
the headlamps to high beam
and it's as if I pulled an organ stop –
black light wobbling
in the wrinkles of the road,
high angelus of trees.

Staple Island Swing

What I hate about love is its dog
EDWIN MORGAN,
'A View of Things'

What I love – the tall clock of thermals, blackbacks
turning on Sunday axles. A guillemot gaping,
mouth like a mussel shell. The grooved bright meat.

What I hate – cormorants –
when there's one chick too many, sprawled
on the rock like an over-loved fuzzy bear.

What I love – in two and threes,
the cormorants' greasy
green heraldries.

What I hate – eyes like sour sweeties.
Holiday cruelties: watching the veins in her calves,
the man watching the woman walking.

What I hate – sickening for a poem,
counting birds into a poem.
What I love – a bird poem.

What I love – a bull seal kippering,
like those fish in red cellophane
we laid on palms to tell fortunes.

What I love – the fantailed terns
adorning your aura
like a devil and an angel.

What I love – the terns giving beak
baksheesh, darning our arms,
sticking our heads like hatpins.

What I love – outrage on the rocks,
a shifting bag of magma, hardening
to a bullseal in the slashed green water.

What I love, the guillemots with their shit tracers,
like me showing off in painty trousers,
playing at being a decorator.

What I love – beaks wagging like metronomes,
bakelite black of cormorants,
the guffy jazz of sea-cliffs.

Hen Pheasant

(for Andrew Miller)

You're clearing moon out of cloud,
scrambling cloud all up
with fingers. But what's her riff,
what's your song for Mrs Mannequin –
the sudden-struck, struck-steel chord
in wet rhodos, who resonates from rain,
who even walks
chromatic, raising a shiver of cock-comets,
compared to whose oilslick
and conker
and silk balaclava
she's just beige and black, coppers
in hot ash. Just moth's underthings.
But gold and steel are your strings,
steel and gold the fine fat mannequin,
all doubled thirds her wings
with hundred haloed eyes.

Sound Test

(for A.M.)

So he plays *Angie*
and holds his breath to the phrase-end.
Panting he lifts his gecko fingertips.

And he plays *Mona Ray* –
his five guitars
getting jilted one by one.

And Angie, mulish, splay-legged
in her swag of skirt
stacks coppers into potential pints.

He silts the air with *Cripple Creek*.
Angie sighs, lays a fingernail,
like a plectrum, across her lips

and Reynardine is heckling
oh slide, bend it, oh who
can give me a fag?

Bushfire, the flare of match to cigarette.

Starring

He says *starring* means the first tick-tack of the chick's beak on the luminous wall. And we are so new I can still call him Centaur. My Centaur is constellation-tall. His honeycomb beard. His dappled back. When it snows, his beard fills with its fourth colour, like the blizzard packs the dark branches.

LORELEI'S LORE

Hey Hey Bo' Weevil. Where's your native home?
SHIRLEY COLLINS,
'Boll Weevil Holler'

NOTE

You might like some background about the siren, Skerryman. There are all these tales about how he was born, and why he ended up as he did – weather stories and creation myths. If you like archetypes, he's the Green Man, a doleful Coyote, the Hanged Man (the martyr), the Devil (the challenge) – a real bag of cats. He's the radio mast on Ronas Hill, the carcass of a stag on a beach in Skye: the discord that makes a pretty scene beautiful. He and Ghosty dance all over Scotland. And whenever he gets near enough to touch, Skerryman – the patron saint of Playing Hard to Get – brings in the cloud, and pulls a white-out down around his shoulders.

The King's Courtyard

What's the drift of coconuts and sultanas the way
he jabs his milkwet fingers into dough
got to do with constellations got to do with real stars
got to do with the suburbs and all
this honeyed Jallaabi of streetlamps? wonders Ghosty,
Girl Racer, fastest Balti in the West. *Ali*, she says,
Ali, is Peshwari sweet?

The moment Ghosty arrives inside her body
the naan is volcanically possessed, and blisters.
Cardamom pitch boatly in the boiling tchai.

And going home she's learning her new reality
where the car is lamp to her genie,
her blood neon with sugar. Thirty pounds
tides back and forth across her dashboard
as she slaloms mini-roundabouts.

The city sky is baked in its own lights
and round and clay as a tandoor,
but Ghosty, shredding the hot naan,
knows streetlamps are beautiful,
they *are*, oh *beautiful*,
they star her face like butter.

Full Walnut Moon

Full Walnut Moon – looks rotten
the way the night is cankered with trees.
Asteroidal houses pocked
with dark panes. Across my headlamps,
a pheasant, Mars-red.

Mornings, they mark my fragile eyes
and ask if he's any good, and I go *oh aye*
and continue my orbit, unmapped,
compiling not transmitting
these garbled messages.

How's he doing then, your man?
My last loving ended
with his diesel engine dwindling,
one hand on the door's frost brass
sensing the night hadn't done with me yet.

Tarantella

If I went to the doctor he'd say strep throat but I tell you your best lurgy is nothing to this. That girl, dancing with the Skerryman, threshing a sheaf of smoke, lanky and lovely as a liquorice bootlace. He'd say *poultice, linctus, calamine. Macallans and lemon. Say ah. Stay out the cold, keep to your bed.* I say, up go the arms, above my head. I hook my hair behind my ears and dance. I jolt my wrists like ju-ju beads.

don't move your lips x x
just shake-uh your hips

The hair slides back on scribbled cheeks and throat's killing, but it's tequila, rotgut, slivovic until storm-doors stutter closed behind Skerryman.
Up go the arms, like cobras.

Marking

Just pressing my cumulus palm
to the white cumulus, just
twinning my hand to lichen.

Stone and skin pressed warmer
than the Kama Sutra's Pressed Kiss.

*

The milk sings.
The fridge curdles.

*

The binbag is too full to tie.
It's been like this for three days.

*

Over knives and forks, crossed,
over scattered parsley,
over blades,
one cautious kiss.

*

Coffee: hot milk, sugar.
I trust you again.

*

Even your few words hum.

*

I let the coffee drip on the paper.
More Jobs Lost.

*

I've not forgotten you cupped
my head to your chest.

*

In Glasgow I stirred up rubbish on the street.
On Skye I was washed up
between a shattered house and a sheep's carcass.

*

All summer you kept me asleep.
I worked in the shop, noticing nothing
but the sun sliding down the blades.

Occasionally I woke with a dirty fresh egg
in each palm, occasionally I found myself
with the price gun in my hand,
sliding another hurt onto the shelf.

*

35,000 feet above Greenland, a raggedy letter, unsent.

*

Night-waking. A letter. Unsent.

*

I regret all those chosen words.
Now I am carefully making mistakes.

*

Breakfast, I continue to think of me.
Selfish heraldry of croissants and jam.

*

I remember inadvertent nakednesses:
your shin,
pecan of your wristbone,
kite of skin where your shirt button slipped.

*

Let's say a time came for you to find me:
a speckled old crab-apple,
passed over by blackbirds
in their evening Jubilate.

Matins

I

The car gives Perthshire the glad-eye of sun,
light frailing the birches' banjo,
accelerates pulse of the knolls to cinnamon.

A crow detaches from the warm road –
chack! starring my windscreen
and the bauble of my soul.

Ten black fingers fold.
A crow falls back
to the dawn-damp road.

II

I drive. All life dodges me.
The early lambs, a cockpheasant
down a furrow.

A horse bends its neck
like a blown brown sail
as I hit along the skittish shore.

And though I race a train
and here it pitches boatly
on the rails,

the sun is plucking at my eyelids,
the red rigs stick in the Firth
like stings.

III

here's a place cracked open to the sky like a dollshouse, here's short reeds glossy as a new-shaved head. Cat's cradle of pylons, pylons shrinking ancestral tree; whatever, we're swung up on the electrical line. A cloud crushed over the forestry, some flossy rain, a tarry taffy choppy loch. Black and white eyebrows raised at the train's mad canter.

IV

I drive. The spicy northern moor:
the Caithness ranches, a raunchy sky,
where wooden fences rot like molars.

Its flank, piebald, currycombed.
A smooth path, tapeworm.
The blue mountains blistering up.

Ghosty? oh, she's gorgeous –
Schiehallion's navel jewel,
swerver of the dour compasses,
a pickle-jar in the cold-press
of the central belt.

Strath Ossian

So on down the strath, a dark hill and a bright mountain and
between the two that old dervish is stirring up clouds, with a
cracked bit of antler from skirmishes of last spring. A right good
mood he's in, grinning like a burst dam, and everything rumpus:
the pan lid chittering, the tea meths-scented. His sour little teeth
crack the last Pink Lady. If he doesn't watch it he'll get kissed,
just for the sake of the bright hill, the dark mountain, the drinking
bitter tea

well what was I meant to do? Kiss that quartzy boulder?

Talking About the Weather

Haar climbs the Voe
and fills the valley's pitcher.
Fence posts barble it.
The red and umber mosses
drink it in.

The waves turn, small
and furious. The clean clothes,
soaked again, wrap arms
about the slippery line.

Haar climbs the track
and a chicken runs across it.

Simmerdim

The sun shows where it intends to rise.
This is the state of the light:
the low hill has plumped up like a loaf,
the road to North Roe sunk dough-deep.

I wish I were the one whose cuticles
are simmerdim, his light smudged lead,
whose promises are full of false summits.

My light is trapped by cattle-grids
and the road's white stitches.
Headlamps waken cats' eyes.
Then the moor falls blind again.
I bend to touch the closed lids.

Simmerdim. Pushes downy heat
into crowns of Collafirth and Ronas,
is ticks and whiskers
and tail-barbs vibrating for a mate.
Its tallow is a curlew's cry –
no call as brash as my torch in this sky –
it has a thousand bubbly pulses
gurgling
          go-go-go-to-bed.

Where I walk a hedgehog freezes,
every grey snaps shut,
each pale withdraws.

A970

Ghosty is Francis Assisi for engines, loves the lot: the starling valves of mopeds, the coltish GTIs. Lorries, awnings slack on knobby hips. For her, the hatchback shies around these Clydesdale tyres. She palms the hot tread above her head.

Now the Girl Racer is the darling of the Sumburgh road, swung up like a diabolo and flourishly caught again. Other cars slide down its line like loveless beads of rain.

Now she splits the rock-candy of the cliff-road, spreading the speed limit through her prism. The miles mount up like lazybeds.

Crying Taing

The peat is cherried with thick water.
I lever out bones like almonds.
From the grass I pick bones like butterflies
with moor-coloured bone-circled eyes.

From bones like orchids, pan-pipes, fans,
I build the ewe kicking out last night at cars
and the small leap of Ronas Voe;
today blood-muzzled, blind.

I pick up a fragment
for every bone in my body.
My fingers as cold as the bones in the grass.
I wind them round a panhandle, a pen.

Fool Moon

On Ronas stands the Skerryman
and winds uncarded clouds
onto barbed wire bobbins.

The sun is behind him.
Moon twitching forward,
placid white-fish
of the murky South.

A trawler spins on its anchor.
The fishfarm begins to thrum.

He crinkles bog mercury
and then palms it. He yanks
a dusk's merino clots –

he winds in the dags, he winds
in constellations and burred
tick stars –

Castor and Pollux,
the Meadow Midden,
tractor iron and baled wire.

Fool Moon Voices

I

She says
and this is my Tommy –
she makes his name
a soft drum.

II

The sheep are terrified by walkers –
they're foam to my breaker,
trickling into the camber, freezing
where I freeze, stiff and salted,
galloping on. One ewe would rather
run her lamb to Sumburgh
than be passed by me.

III

Sunset – loose on its bolt
the layby sign throbs the place
called Crying Taing.

The post box blushes,
speaks starling.

IV

I said to Tommy
(who was shifting stone)
whatcha doing
and he said *playing*
at Nelson Mandela
what does it look like?

V

Fratres in my headphones
on the radio mast road –
catgut, horsehair,
padded hammers.
My breath, my gong heart.
Long phrase of hot tarmac.

VI

Fethaland, the two oceans
are metres apart
and desperate for each other –

the greasy green feathers
of the North Sea, the reaching
brown kelps of the Atlantic.

The Gannet and Skerryman

*How was Shetland made? This version shows why a gannet's head
is stained like a smoker's fingers, and why Skerryman is always cold.*

Gannet's greedy. Or some folk, seeing the boats come in with half-
catches, say *starving*. And Gannet knows the last big halibut is sculling
around the ocean floor. He dives, you know how, a falling sword.
Screwing down through the water, he gapes his beak and snaps it
shut. But he snips open the seabed and lava elbows out to steam his
skull, and piles out in triple chins, and kicks out – lava on
lava until there crowns an island and a shivering mannie: Skerry-
man, pushed prematurely from the hot earth's gut; sorrowful,
shivering and basalt-black.

Praise-Poem

You close them together in the bud-coat of your palms. You talk about whiteness. Like Tommy, when I say I'll help with the walling. *No no, your hands will be too tender.*

What, will they hatch a blue milk, magnolias?

My hands, my familiars, first vanity since Dad brought out the smallest hammer and folded my fingers round it, then the second smallest, then a sanding block and plane. The genie drawn out of a Calorgas blowtorch.

Waking with you my feet are leafed arch to sole, a tidy seal's, and my fists hard under my shoulders. *My hard woman.* I force you to split my hands. Full of roosting blood, each finger. Palm lined with Shepherd's Warning.

XIV Temperance

Harmonics – a starling
whistling, diode skylark
scrolling radio stations

sheep speaking the New Lamb
condensed black shadow
of his white dam.

You have to move more slowly
round the small moment
you have to move more small-ly.

The anchor-rope plumb
from his belly
the blood rust beneath the tail.

Tinily constellations creep the night
and I orbit the still ewe
and her upwards-butting moon.

III Empress

And how is she beautiful –
the one who rises from marsh-marigolds
and with shining fingers
tugs ringpulls
and mussel-shells
from hair made blue with the peat's oil?

She's the only one who will stand up
to the north-easterly, a viking wind
with a skua for a figurehead.
She breaks it on her brow, splits
the bull-necked bruisy one into skeins,
to graze round lambs
                              crazy bellied.

When the Empress clambers from her couch
a ewe dares stand,
towing in a transparent dragnet, stuffed
with the gauze grey knuckles
of another damp Pan.

Gigi in the Rockpools

Ortolans should be cut in two, with one quick stroke of the knife and
no grating of the blade on the plate. Bite up each half. The bones
don't matter. Go on eating while you answer my question, but don't
talk with your mouth full. You must manage it. If I can, you can.
GIGI,
Colette

This gale. Remember Gigi's chin gripped
in nut-jewelled fingers and tilted,
throat eyed for pearls. South, the Grand-dam,
North, a quavery salty old sook
but still a patriach.

And this blue, how it smalls
it, how it brightens, clipped in strings
in her vanity case; how the old satin-backs
scan the billows, the crowds of gale.

I'm a rudder sinewed to these two winds,
tugged his way her way
on my painted pin.

*

Gigi turns her voice to yolk and royal jelly,
but look at her palms, comb-rough, quietly
pulling-to the gate (beyond the dark byre)
weaving blue twine in an infinity sign,
tugging tight the knot that swells sealed
in rain.

*

I sleep till midday, right down to a low-tide me,
hair condensed, spine an iron chain,
legs sunk and feet sunk into silt.

Yesterday my shirts filled with hoodoo gusts
from the East; now they're knotted like lambs,
wrung out. Water creeps the window
and pools at the pane's foot.

Gigi it's a month
since anyone's touched me.

*

A sheep pioneers the beach's lobe,
drags and sucks a seaweed swag.
Gigi's feet are mollusc-cold,
cheeks painted in the Pierrot vogue.
Lace climbs her throat

barnacle tight
barnacle slow.

Iamb

And when in days or weeks the wind drops,

       I'll give up my raggedy herding

  walk warm and slow along the road, gathered about by breath.

     Let it veer under the rusted tractor.

    Let it return, lamb-shadow, butting.

           Canter ahead of my slow step.

And when the wind drops, my ears will lose their squint wings.

  I'll flinch for no skua or passing car.

     There'll be no waking   exhausted from flying,

   my good silt marrow settled home in bone again.

         Each hill take on again its load.

   The moor billow a sheet of birds.

Thrimilce – Isbister

*The Anglo-Saxons called [May] thrimilce, because then cows
can be milked three times a day.*
BREWER'S PHRASE AND FABLE

Cheddared, the light sealed
in rind of dry road;
bloom and sheen of the ditches
I've been dreaming all this life;
the close-quilled irises
rooted dense and deep
as flight feathers.

Recognition rises –
cream in a tilted pitcher.

XXI The World

Leaving, pull sulky feet like lollipops
from the forty lochans, the forty-one skies.
Taffy they are in the rich blue
for which triptych brushes are poked under cloud.
A crowd of marsh-leaves shake their streaked tongues.

Nortlaand – more numerous than ewes,
than ganglion roads in a thousand voes.
Neither Swinister nor Eshaness nor Crying Taing
must take the brunt of my love.

No I won't forget the gate but tie it loosely,
a plywood wing
to thud my sternum when the wind is up.

she comes with dogs
in her slipstream –
a bent wing of hounds –
a Warm Front.

Dog-days

There was and there wasn't a summer and it hung half-clipped from the mountain's scraped shoulders. Sun just a stain, a fleecy stain. Months ago, the tup.

In the Cuillin, an old rescue dog chafes its wet neck on Sgurr nan Gillean. It's Skerryman's hound, cross between a haar and a husky. He found it locked in a transit van, shit and a dead sheep, coat matted to daub and wattle. Three Days, *Good Dog*, not barking.

There was and there wasn't a summer when the mountains were like stone-chipped teeth. And Skerryman's finger, unhooked from the soft gape, let cloud furl up to heal the hurt gums. *And if the dog's not died, they're still there now.*

Orchid Dog

Orchid Dog swells at dusk,
claiming the clapboard moor,
its chambered cairns and basalt topknots.

He raises a field-full of white gulls,
shadow bruising a bloated sheep.
He jerks and swings a mouthful of rank ribbons.

Orchid Dog is soaked and shoulder-deep.
The burn hanks his hair, bares
his belly-suede and coded nipples.

He hunts a flooded vole
he'll never kill and polkas on it
jumping on and off its hot ember.

I scuff wet grasses for a rock anvil.
He rolls the wet plush
in the rose and chocolate corals of his grin.

A835

In sun the moor turns harlequin and whisky sours.
The road runs down to single-track.
In rain, headlamps bloom chrysanthemum
but she sleeps on, sways
with lax complexity of bladderwrack.

Full Sheeptick Moon

Weedy drymouth Feb
                    LES MURRAY,
                    'Feb'

An hour at high-tide,
edgy patience with the fankle-line
of July, bail-arm jammed,
hooks gripped in the grind.

A ribbon teaseweed
to flutter my spinner,
greenly.

*

Dimps of season July,
new dot to dot galaxies of freckle,
clear dabs of midge honey;

July, our sun
in wee wet bursts
that bless the heads of orchids'
ragatag magenta.

A raised red season
but nerveless as the quenched wineglasses.

Woke at four to their fingerprints
and pale mouths, a tremulous
cooling hour,

watching the lighthouse
smear the haar.

*

Now summer is the season
of clingings-on, high dithering grasses,
this-an-that of mackerel.

Summer sky peeled from your soles
in grey crescents.

The swallows come, wings
black boomerang,
loaded with ticks
and pearly winter weathers.

her bruise – a passing
weather – swells
like cumulo-nimbus
on my lower lip.

One That Got Away

And our pure pure mackerel time
came in a run at the loch-head.
Hooked, its Chinese-red gills spread,

tinning my palm with rose and lightning
before it made a break for it,
spannering the cracked granite,
and we were swearing, and begging
the fish to worship the line.

My fault it was a blink season
in a brackish summer. Too tenderly priested,
it barely lived
                or died. Oh, *other*

Julys drummed my line –
we landed bronzes, hunchback coleys
like lucky pennies,

and the wee boys begged
to make the killing wallop.

Song of Parts

This is how the catch is gutted –
you diddle the knife down fatty silver,
fingernail-deep, the broad blade's tip.
Slow burgundies stain the enamel sink.
Mackerel hoop and harden in your grip.
With tugsome bravery you yank
the gut-end, coda of a bloodless old song;
the silty fruits coddled away;
the clean fish and its swimbladder,
like a tigerlily,
                    on the cutting board

her smile's like the flight
of a siskin – dash dot dash dot
--- -.. .-.. it
grips her mouth with tiny claws
teetering

Hey Hey Mr Blue

Skerryman's in that blue shirt, makes everything like Indian summer, unbelievable it'll ever end. What's beautiful? The hack-uddered cattle, sun like gold-top on their bulging flanks. My arms, the swaggering right sunburnt, a python on the wound-down window. The pale left, scooping the car round fruity bends. Every blazing day is like the old songs and tonic water, the grasses tipsy, starlings like crochet rests on the telegraph's stave. Imagine Skerryman, in his nostalgia shirt. Hey *Hey* Mr Blue. I beat time in the cidery grasses.

And Skerryman goes

                        right-o, time I was getting on

and moves your hand, and zips his fly, and antlered a silent Harrier zips the blue sky, trailing a streamer of ROAR.

Ullinish

A racing sky
patched and manic as the next croft's
untethered Bess.

A cat bolts from its throne of rocks.

Ghosty's Almanac

How many seas? Engines boiling water to black liquorice, the oily harbour at cracking point, the sea shrugging its itchy skins. A sea with soft hiccups. A sea swinging up above the ferry windows.

How many peaks? Eaval, Dearg, a blue mountain, the Red Mountain, pinned to the land like weird wild brooches. How much sheep grass? Fields-full, rusting.

How many pints? How many drams gave me the mythic wildness on an empty belly? How many gallons of Unleaded, the petrol cap like a black clover on the car's roof? Fort William, raining, pumps green and glowing the wet summer. In Struan, your man in the wrinkly tin, filling the tank with gurgling breath and trying to steer the conversation onto udders.

XII The Hanged Man – Assynt

They said *it'll be a pretty ride*
through the Minch at this
time of year, Mr S.,
and (laughing dirtily)
better once you land in Stornoway.

How did I fail to recognise
my mountains from the sea?
Suilven – the bear's rump.
My Polly.

Every seventh wave wallops the hull
and shackled cars – reminds me
of the cattle on the Westray boat
deck streaked
with salt and shit – hooing
from the iron cradles.

And there by the lifeboat
is the Ghosty-girl.
Her white face. Her blue cagoule.
A saltire, stripped.

Every seventh wave
thumps the steel bodhran
oh man
– I wish
you would let me be.

Feel better in Stornoway,
well enough for lunch. Chicken chow mein
from the businessman's menu
and a mug of tea. oh jee

sus –
the shifting summits,
the hoisin sea.

well didn't I drive until the wet road
held more light than the sky,
didn't I drive
like Hänsel and Gretel
had dropped a trail of cats' eyes?

Barm Brack

The smoked glass ashtray is trembling with rainwater. My palm caps a mug, is printed by the hot ring of steam. The engine, tink-tinking. The gusted landscape, still shrinking: the mountains riding the bronco moor, the mountains chucked across Assynt like jacks. Stac Pollaidh. Suilven, the Tea-Loaf, the big rock candy mountain. Twelve ounces, ten ounces, seven. Dried fruit, soaked through the night in tea and brown sugar. Flour and an egg. It's done when a flat knife slides out clean. That's it. And though the skin of his neck is malt and smooth, this is what you have to do. Cut the crust of the mountain they call Sugarloaf. Out flies Skerryman, wi' four and twenty wagtails.

where is she?
not in the old bath
where cattle drink
from the sky's green iris.

0 The Fool – Skye

May you find your spraints of claw
and coiled damp tail and splintered bone
and brochs of snails and seeds of fruits
          all fortune-cookied.

May the light land
every day differently on your bird-table

mackerel black
                    mackerel silver

ALMANACS

Trespass/Saturnalia

I

She can't wait to cross
the barbed wire.

Resurrection of the Green Knight!
Green floods her, gloom welshes her.

Her numb fingers
are buzzing with plankton.

II

Her stick stabs mulch
as deep as snow; she drops
it, hangs on holly to cut holly.

III

She wears small wounds for weeks,
a bruise lashed to her leg like a flint to a spear.

IV

Pie-eyed with danger,
a pantomime burglar,
she banishes me
to distant scant-berried trees.

V

*I can't remember
the last time
I was in a wood.*

Unfledging

I raise Paisley wounds,
spill yellow pollen of fat.
This is reversing time, like a vandal

who scores shellac blooms
from a soundbox, tightens to snapping
the strings of a lute.

As if I scraped a poem's lard
from vellum. As brattish
as kicking a cat.

In pale skin are magnolia buds:
the muscles that worked wings,
but I've undone the wings,

gripping each pinion
as if to slide home the marriage ring
and never dream of flying again;

I've plucked the eyed, seed feathers,
the chicky down, the fine human hair
like first casing of mushroom spawn,

the long quills that striped across
the evening sun this week,
trembling in the rainstorm's target.

Drawing

It takes two hours and my family sits with me,
to witness the punch of shot in the fluted thigh
that I dig out like a peppercorn.

Tasha fetches newspapers, folds away
wet feathers. Mum teaches me algebra.
Minus (spurs, coccyx, head, feet) = meat.

She makes me angry by crying,
briefly, a brief shame,
                    a burst of shot.

Lida Aerra / Joytime / June

June, cool dusk wipes the field's eye
and tugging green wheat I'm small again,
milking rain from my tapering plaits.

June, bum on the stile, *tictictic*
becomes cantering fox. The hedgerow slopes
from my shoulders;

a yoke to hang a poem and a pail.

Hooymaand / Hay Month / July

She walks until wheat's green lingo
becomes a nanny English of rusks
and tsks.

She walks whilst gummy-eyed
the field looks up to the moon
as if at the gleaming shins of women –

she walks till there's holes in her corduroy
and her fur shows, wry
and grey as the beard of a sage.

Harvest makes her brood about her age:
her linen albicans,
heart's moth clattering between underwires.

July rain! She stomps bald continents
amongst the grain. *You wanted a poem.*
Happy harvest home.

Thermidor

In the heat you can see her heart
beat in her back – nudging
her fragile teeshirt –
a gecko
on a scorching wall.

.

She tells me the way
she wants things done.
We'll use up the twin-tub's rinse water –
then haul from the butt
the neglected, treacly rain.

.

it'd be a relief
to sweat

a little ship
traverses her eyebrow's
painted meridian

Fructidor / September

your voice-note dented
like a dropped tin kettle

something in your eyes
tarnished

your voice changed
jerked backwards
along the time-line

then tuned back up
through Doric and Aeolian

tin strings dragging on a tough bridge
tin strings hauled
onto dense bone pegs

I held my hand to your scalp
and blood overran my palm
fell down my arm
in hot tails

I was proud of it
commonplace rare
like home-made jam

say, medlar, rare fruit
and rare word, common-place
precious

just kept coming
found it later in my nails
and the cracks in my skin

overflow as the creeper
you had me cut last week

died like a second sunset
in next door's tree.

M74 Glasgow to Carlisle

(for Anna, for Tom)

> *For what you have and haven't done, the same regret.*
> YANNIS RITSOS

1. Used to be arch about Lanarkshire, all iron and bile
2. then crook of silthills aroused my girl, as I drove her through Sanquhar.
3. I showed her a kestrel, pendant from the sky's collarbone.
4. Looking for a place to love, all the hills subsided.
5. I didn't ask, *how is it with you now?*
6. Watched cows break the field's crust, my shoulderblades to oak

7. Used to be arch about Abington, the river, the liverspots of the moor.
8. Men in overalls keeping their distance, start to whistle made-up tunes.
9. Thinking about a girl at school, who, hugged, trembled.
10. Her arms behind her, less an embrace than a curtsey.
11. I knew she dreaded it, but couldn't bear the cringing space.
12. But how do we dare?

13. Windfarm, pylons, it does me good to see you.
14. Sundown, car's shadow twirling like a hula skirt
15. Evening, headlamps, I wouldn't live in another time:
16. the big bright beasts, overtaking as slow as oxen,
17. their panting tarpaulin!

18. What I'm guilty of – *I wouldn't live in another time.*
19. What I'm guilty of – not asking, *how is it with you now?*
20. What I'm guilty of – but how do we dare?

Downpour

the man paws the doormat,
the girl trots across like a flamenca
reaching eventually
the clean dry floor

Ryecroft, November

(for Tashy)

My gums are like this field
when I dream about spitting teeth,
muddy and crimped with pot shards:
canines with starburst of cracked lacquer,
the long yellow years of horses,
the Toby-jug molars winking a woad lily,
an ultramarine bridge.

sanctus

the nightlight angels
      the Teasmade angels
            the radiant angels bucking

then putting on again the habitual clothes
      the High Street angels
            the battledress angels

the angels crossing their wings of tin
      taking grid-reference
            from the angels with walkie-talkies

the interleaved angels
      the angels in reins
            the angels with webcam stigmata

the mighty cog angels of braid and feather
      the pivot Jibreels
            the treadmill seraphim

the swinging cross the swaying cross
      the rising cross of beaten iron
            the angels with reluctant winches

the angels lost in clocks and watches
      daydreaming
            the angels doubting angels

the angels spitting breath
      the angels spitting vodka sorrow
            the angels risking juice and water

the thinmilk Bodhisattvas
      the hushed, dumpling Bodhissatvas
            the angels spitting beak-fed manna

the insomniac angels redrawing lines
    the angels carroting urban soil
        the angels letting the sky lie fallow

the angels retreating from the woeful steel
    the molten chorale

        the angels in diaspora

Notes to the Almanacs

Hen Pheasant

comet: dialect word for a male pheasant.

Bert Jansch's album *Avocet* includes *Avocet, Lapwing, Bittern, Kingfisher, Osprey* and *Kittiwake.* But no pheasants.

Sound Test

Angie, Mona Ray, Reynardine: more Jansch titles.

Tarantella

> *'don't move your lips*
> *just shake your hips...'*
> ROLLING STONES, 'Shake Your Hips'

Full Walnut Moon, Fool Moon, Full Sheeptick Moon

After the convention of naming full moons according to crops and seasonal tasks. *The Farmer's Almanac* includes these:

> January – Full Old Moon
> February – Full Hunger Moon
> March – Full Crust Moon
> May – Full Milk Moon

http://www.almanac.com/astronomy/moonnames.php

Lorelei's Lore

Lorelei, siren who lured sailors to their deaths on the Rhine.

> *'She used to love in a strange kind of fashion*
> *with lots of hey-ho-de-ho-hi-de-hi'*
> IDA GERSHWIN, 'Lorelei'

Full Moon Voices

Fratres: Instrumental variations by Arvo Pärt.

XXI The World

Nortlaand: Northmavine, the northern segment of mainland Shetland.

'Nortlaand, I see dy
Lang stem o red ert
Creepin laek a finger
Owre da watter o Saint Magnus'
ROBERT ALAN JAMIESON, 'Shoormal'

Hey Hey Mr Blue

from 'Mr Blue Sky', Electric Light Orchestra.

Thermidor

Thermidor: 'The eleventh month of the French Republican calendar ...from Gr. *therme*, heat; *doron*, a gift.' *Brewer's Dictionary of Phrase and Fable*.

Trespass / Saturnalia

Saturnalia: 'The ancient Roman festival of SATURN, celebrated on 19 December...a time of freedom from restraint, merrymaking, and often riot and debauchery.' *Brewer's Dictionary of Phrase and Fable*.

M74 Glasgow to Carlisle

'for what we have and haven't done...': this is # 215 in Yannis Ritsos' collection of 336 short poems.

www.ingramcontent.com/pod-product-compliance
Lightning Source LLC
Jackson TN
JSHW080854211224
75817JS00002B/42